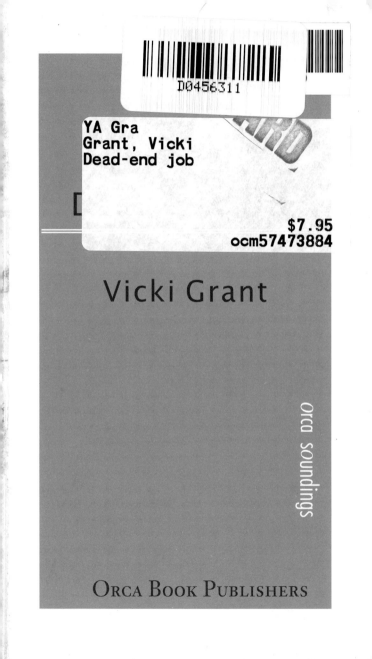

Vicki Grant

orca soundings

ORCA BOOK PUBLISHERS

Copyright © 2005 Vicki Grant

National Library of Canada Cataloguing in Publication Data

Grant, Vicki
Dead-end job / Vicki Grant.

(Orca soundings)
ISBN 1-55143-378-8

I. Title. II. Series.

PS8613.R367D42 2005   jC813'.6   C2005-900339-1

Summary: When it turns out that the boy Frances has met at her job
working the nightshift is a stalker, she realizes she may be in serious danger.

First published in the United States, 2005
Library of Congress Control Number: 2005920401

Orca Book Publishers gratefully acknowledges the support for its
publishing programs provided by the following agencies:
the Government of Canada through the Department of Canadian
Heritage's Book Publishing Industry Development Program (BPIDP),
the Canada Council for the Arts, and the British Columbia Arts Council.

Cover design: Lynn O'Rourke
Cover photography: Firstlight.ca

Orca Book Publishers   Orca Book Publishers
PO Box 5626, Stn. B.   PO Box 468
Victoria, BC Canada   Custer, WA USA
V8R 6S4   98240-0468

08 07 06 05 • 5 4 3 2 1

Printed and bound in Canada.
Printed on 30% post-consumer recycled paper,
processed chlorine-free using vegetable, low VOC inks.

In memory of Meg Richardson,
who loved stories and who loved us.

Chapter One

There was something really weird about that bag of cheese doodles. It was too fat at the bottom or too pointy at the corners or something. I stared at it for ages, but I couldn't figure out what was wrong with it. It was making me crazy.

I grabbed my hair and screamed.

Someone said, "Are you all right?"

I nearly jumped out of my skin. I hadn't even heard the guy come in. I tried to casually put my hand over my drawing. I didn't want him to see it. I said, "Oh. Yeah. I'm fine. Can I help you?"

He put a chocolate bar on the counter. He said, "I just came in to buy this." Then he smiled in a way he probably thought was cute and whispered, "But now I'd really like to see your picture too."

I sort of smiled back. He was a customer after all. I didn't want to be rude. But I didn't want to encourage him either—especially since he was nowhere near as hot as he thought he was. He was just sort of normal. Your average eighteen-year old with the hoodie, the jeans, and the earphones hooked around his neck. He was sort of pale, sort of skinny and could have used a shave too. (I only noticed that because I was trapped behind the counter looking at him. Normally I wouldn't have noticed him at all.)

"Pleeeease?" he said. He gave me that cheesy smile again. This was getting embarrassing. Even more embarrassing than me screaming.

I said, "Ah, no. I don't think so." I pulled a box of bubble gum over my drawing.

"C'mon. Don't be shy," he said and tried to take a peek.

"That will be $1.07 for the bar," I said. I covered the rest of the picture with a copy of the week's Lotto numbers.

"Okay, okay." He shrugged like it was no big deal. "Here's one and a quarter. Keep the change."

Oooh. All that charm and a big tipper too. I threw the money in the cash and then we both just sort of stood there. I found it really awkward, but it didn't seem to bug him at all. He took a bite of his Krispy Bits and said, "Mmmm. Good bar." As if I had something to do with it. He leaned against the counter until he finished eating. Then he wiped his hand on his jacket and said, "Well, I guess I better get going."

No kidding, I thought.

"Thanks for coming in," I said.

He was on his way out past the magazine rack when the phone rang. What a relief. It was almost midnight. It had to be my boyfriend. I crouched down behind the cigarette rack and acted like the perfect little receptionist.

"Highway Buyway Convenience Store. This is Frances. How may I direct your call?"

Leo *demanded* to speak with the head of Customer Relations immediately! He was appalled at the shabby treatment he'd received that day from one of our salespeople. He didn't catch her name, but he could describe her. She had scraggy blond hair, brown old-lady glasses and size eleven feet. (It sounded a lot like me, but I wasn't going to admit to anything.)

According to Leo, she had refused to sneak out of biology class with him that day. He'd even promised to give her a biology lesson himself in the back of his "way cool" 1985 Impala. If this behavior did not stop, he said, he would be forced to report the Highway Buyway to the Better Business Bureau!

We had been goofing around like that for a while when I heard someone in the store. I figured it was the owner coming in to do the nightshift. I whispered, "See you at the usual time," and hung up. Mr. Abdul's a nice guy and everything, but he still doesn't want me flirting with my boyfriend on company time.

I hopped up from behind the counter and said "Hi!" in this really bouncy cheerleader voice. I wanted to sound like your ideal employee. The type of person who just loves spending her Friday nights restocking the cigarette shelves.

"Well, hello there!" It was Mr. Krispy Bits again.

Great.

"Can I help you?" I said.

"Yeah. Mind if I stay here for a few minutes? It's really starting to rain outside."

I did mind, but what could I say?

"I guess not," I said and actually started to restock the cigarettes.

He said, "You don't have to sound so happy about it. I mean, I could help you."

Oh right. Just what I wanted.

"No thanks," I said. "This'll only take a second and my shift's almost over anyway."

He snorted. I'm not kidding. "I don't mean help stocking the shelves!" I turned toward the low-tar section and rolled my eyes. Like he's too good to stock shelves.

"I mean, I could help with your drawing," he said.

I heard this shushing sound. I turned around just in time to see him pull the picture out from under the bubble gum box.

"Hey!" I said.

He had my drawing in his hands and was studying it as if he was some kind of major art expert.

"This is good," he said, nodding.

I was mad now. "How would you know?" I took a swipe at the drawing but he jumped out of the way.

"Ever heard of Tom Orser?" he said.

"Yeah. So what?" In a little town like this, who wouldn't know Tom?

I took another swipe at my drawing.

"He's my father."

"Sure," I said. Like I was going to fall for that one. Tom Orser is this really rich wildlife artist. He lives in an amazing house way out on the cliff at East Green Harbor. He's about sixty and his wife's about thirty. They have two little girls. Zorah, who likes salt-and-vinegar chips, and Stella, who prefers all-dressed.

"He comes in here all the time," I said. "He doesn't have a son."

Krispy Bits went even paler than he already was. I figured I had him.

"Not by this wife," he said. His face had gone really serious. "I'm the product of wife number one. The one who had to work to support the starving artist."

He wasn't kidding. I didn't know what to say. I could hardly get mad at him now. It was really uncomfortable. Just to be nice I said, "When did they split up?"

"I was about eight. Tom started making money and decided to trade the old lady in for a newer model. A swimsuit model, in fact. That would be Sacha, wife number two. They had three kids. Then he dumped her for someone prettier. Margo got fat after the second baby, so he left her for the wife he has now."

He had this fake smile on his face. I had a horrible feeling he was going to start to cry.

"Did you know he had other wives?" he asked.

"Ah...no," I said. I was starting to wish I'd just let him take the stupid picture in the first place.

"So how did you know he didn't have a son then?"

He had me there. This seemed really painful for him. I mumbled some apology-type thing. I thought he was going to stomp out of the store, but he just shrugged.

"Hey, don't feel bad," he said. "Most of the time Tom acts like he doesn't know he has a son either. Tell him Devin came into your store and watch what he does. He'll go, 'Who's he?' I'm serious. Try it next time he comes in."

He laughed and handed me back my picture.

"It's good, Frances. I mean it," he said. "You just made the bag a little too short on the left side."

I looked down at the picture.

Damn. He was right.

I was just going to thank him when something hit me. I looked up.

"Hey," I said. "How do you know my name?"

He didn't answer. Somehow he'd managed to disappear just before Mr. Abdul walked in the door.

Chapter Two

We were driving home after my shift that night and I was telling Leo about what happened. He couldn't believe the stuff about Tom dumping all those women.

He said, "Let me see if I got this right. After he left his first wife, Tom had seven kids with three different women? In, like, what? Ten years?"

He burst out laughing. "The man's a love god! I hope I'm doing that good when I'm ninety."

"Tom's not ninety," I said.

"Okay then. I hope I'm doing that good when I *look* ninety."

I cracked up. We both cracked up. That was mean. But it's true. Tom's this little round guy with a white ponytail and shorts that come up to his armpits. No one around town could believe he managed to get himself one tall, beautiful wife. They were going to die when they found out he'd had four.

Anyway, we were having a great time together and so I just kept blabbing away. I told Leo about Devin grabbing the picture and seeing right off what was wrong with it. I said the guy sure had a good eye. I was really impressed.

That was my big mistake.

Leo slammed his mouth shut and just stared at the road the whole rest of the way home.

I hate it when he gets like that. All I did was make one little comment about a guy having a good eye.

But that's not what Leo hears.

Leo hears: "The guy is really artistic so he must be really smart too. And, by the way, did I mention that you're not? You're just a big dumb hockey player who wants to stay in Lockeport for the rest of his life and take over his dad's garage. That's why I'm going to dump you for some complete stranger."

Which just goes to prove that Leo really is a moron.

Ever since I decided I want to go away to art college next year, he's had this big chip on his shoulder. Like I was doing it to make him look stupid or something. Nothing I could say made any difference. Leo *is* smart. I've always said that. Not in school, maybe. (Okay, not in school, for sure.) But he's smart in other ways. He can fix anything. He's got common sense. He's really funny. He understands stuff about people and the world that a lot of kids with good marks just don't get.

And if all that isn't enough, he's a whole lot hotter than a dorky girl like me deserves.

I love the guy. Even when he's being an idiot.

Part of me really wanted to let him have it right then. He was acting like such a baby. But the other part of me was just too tired. I was working hard at school. I was working hard getting a portfolio together for Art College. And I was working at the Highway Buyway. Frankly, at one o'clock in the morning, I didn't have any energy left to work at our "relationship."

It pissed me off to think that I even had to.

Leo pulled into my driveway and left the car running. I looked at him. I wanted to say, "C'mon, Leo. Don't be like that. I couldn't care less about Devin." But Leo turned his head away. He started drumming his fingers on the steering wheel like I was wasting his precious time. Like I was supposed to just hurry up and apologize.

I couldn't do that.

I sighed and said, "See ya."

He said, "Yeah." Then he punched the dashboard hard.

I got out. He gunned it down the driveway.

The light in my parents' room went on.

Great.

Two more people mad at me for something I didn't do.

Chapter Three

Leo didn't call all the next day.

I guess I could have phoned, but what was I going to say? Talking to him right then would only have made things worse. He'd want me to say sorry. And I'd want to tell him what a jerk he was.

I figured I'd give it a day to blow over. I tried to study for history. I tried to do a landscape for my portfolio. I tried to read a trashy magazine, but I couldn't even concentrate on that. This thing with Leo was really bugging me. I ended up just hanging around the house and picking stupid fights with everyone until it was time to leave for work at six o'clock.

I was surprised to see Mr. Abdul there. Normally his wife does the dayshift, but he told me she was having trouble with her pregnancy. The doctor didn't want her on her feet that day. Mr. Abdul must have been bagged by the time I arrived. He'd been working for eighteen hours straight.

I guess that's why the place was such a disaster. The shelves hadn't been stocked all day, and the snack counter was a mess. I didn't care. The evening shift is always pretty slow. Every so often a trucker will come in for some bad coffee, or a tourist will stop to ask how far it is to civilization. (Answer: Far.) Other than that, it's pretty dead. That's the whole reason I took the job. It gave me plenty of time to draw or—I hate to admit it—daydream about Leo.

That night, though, I didn't feel like doing either. I was glad to have shelves to clean. I'd spent enough time sulking.

I pulled my hair up with an old elastic band and got to work. I went totally crazy. It was like I was thinking: *I'll show Leo who he's messing with! I'll clean the store! That'll teach him.*

It didn't make sense, but it sure got me going. I restocked the candy section. I tidied the magazines. I swept the floor, cleaned the windows and scraped the scuzz off the inside of the microwave. By the time I got around to scrubbing out the dairy fridge, I was sweating like a pig.

I was down on my knees with a J-cloth, scooping this gross pink sludge off the bottom rack, when something clammy touched my neck.

I screamed. I didn't even look. I just hurled the wet rag at whatever it was that touched me.

There was a splat. Then someone swore.

I turned around. My wild throw had got Devin right in the head.

"You scared me!" I said.

"Well, we're even then," he went, "because you scared me too."

I had to laugh. Both times I saw the guy I screamed. Screaming might have been reasonable if he was a big ex-con biker type. But Devin looked so harmless—especially with half his face dripping pink goo.

He wiped his eye with the back of his hand. "What is this stuff?" he said. "It stinks!"

"Cherry yogurt—or at least it was. Once upon a time."

"Oh, gross." He gagged. "Serves me right for sneaking up on you I guess."

"Yes, it does," I said.

"Do I have to leave it on my face so that everyone knows I've been bad? Or can I use your washroom?"

I'm not really supposed to let customers use the washroom, but this was different. I was sort of to blame. I led him out through the stockroom to the back of the store.

The bathroom's about the size of a phone booth. It seemed even smaller, though, because it was stuffed with cardboard boxes we couldn't put anywhere else. I went to take the boxes out so Devin would have some room. He followed me right in. I turned around to leave and there we were, squished together face-to-face in this grubby little washroom. Somehow he seemed to find that romantic.

It was so awkward. My hands were full of boxes and I had nowhere to move.

He smiled at me and said, "So…"

I wasn't sure what he meant. I didn't want to find out.

I said, "You're right. That stuff doesn't smell very nice, does it?" That made him back off a bit. I wiggled past him. "Would you mind leaving the window open when you're done?" I asked.

Chris Cooper from Diamond Taxi was waiting at the counter when I came out. He bought his Jersey Milk bar and then hung around talking for a while. He's a nice guy, so I didn't mind.

Chris had left to pick up a customer and I was back wiping shelves by the time Devin came out. He was all clean and shiny.

"Boo," he said.

"Not funny," I said.

He nodded. "Oh-oh. Now I have to say sorry for something else." He looked embarrassed. "Believe it or not, that's the only reason I came in today. To say sorry for last night."

"That's okay," I said.

"No, it's not," he said. "I was being a jerk. I shouldn't have taken your drawing."

"It's okay," I said.

"I've got an excuse," he said. "I was tired. I'd been hitchhiking for a week to get here and I was nervous about seeing my dad again. Then I ran into a pretty girl and I acted like an idiot."

"That's okay," I said. "It's no big deal." I just wanted him to stop talking about it.

"It's a big deal to me, though," he said. "That's why I brought you these."

He pulled a box out of his jacket pocket. It was a full set of pastels. Really, really good French pastels. He put them on the counter. I couldn't believe it.

I shook my head. This wasn't right.

"You can't give me those!" I pushed them back toward him. "They're too expensive!"

"Don't worry about that," he said. "I'm actually okay for money."

I looked at his scruffy jacket. He noticed.

"Okay, so I don't look it!" He laughed. "But it's the truth! I've got lots of money. In fact, that's why I came out here. I wanted to tell my dad I just signed a big recording deal."

"Really?" It was probably rude of me to look so surprised.

"Yeah. Really. I figured Tom might be happy to see me now that I'm a...success." He made quotation marks in the air with his fingers. He rolled his eyes like "what a joke."

"In fact, I was going to go over to his place today but..." He shrugged. "I chickened out. I went into the city instead to buy you these."

He pushed the pastels back toward me. "C'mon. I made a special trip just for you."

I sighed. I just looked at them. I didn't know what to do. I felt bad for the guy. I couldn't take them. But I didn't want to hurt his feelings either. It sounded like he'd had a rough enough day already.

"Please," I said. "That's really nice, but I'd rather you keep them."

"Nah. I don't want them," he said. "I bought myself something even better." He took the tiniest digital camera you ever saw out of his pocket. "Cool, huh?"

He came around the counter and showed me what it could do. I had to lean in close to see.

"Don't move," he said.

He held the camera out at arm's length and took a picture of us. The flash surprised me. I laughed.

"This'll be good," he said. "Your hair looks great like that."

"You're such a liar," I said.

His head snapped around.

"Did you call me a liar?" He had this totally psycho look on his face.

"I…I just meant you're lying about my hair!" I said. "It's all sweaty and tangled. It looks terrible. I mean it. I wasn't trying to upset you."

He laughed. It was like nothing had happened. His face had gone completely back to normal. He said, "I'm not upset. I was just kidding around. And anyway, I think your hair looks great like that. See?" He showed me the picture. He had one arm around my shoulder and was smiling at me. I was laughing. "You look gorgeous."

I didn't want to call him a liar again. I just smiled and said, "Ah. It's almost midnight. I've got to do my cash, get ready to go."

"I'll help if you want. I could sweep or whatever."

I didn't have time to answer. I saw a car turning off the highway.

A 1985 Impala.

That's all I needed right then.

Leo catching me with Devin.

Chapter Four

"It's my boyfriend," I said. I must have gone totally white.

"Are you all right?" he asked.

I looked out the window. Thank God Leo was having trouble with first gear again. It gave me a couple of extra seconds to figure out what to do.

"Yeah. Fine," I said, but I was lying. I wasn't fine at all.

I heard the engine turn off. I panicked. I said, "Don't let him see you!"

Devin asked, "Why?"

I pushed him. "You've got to go!"

I didn't have time to explain. It didn't matter. Devin was suddenly smiling at me, like we had some big private joke.

"Oh, I get it," he said.

The car door closed.

"The bathroom window!" I whispered. "Go out the bathroom window!"

Devin winked and ducked down behind the Pringles display. I heard the door creak open. I stuffed the pastels beneath the counter and pretended to straighten the lottery tickets.

I don't know how Leo missed seeing Devin, but he did. He walked right past the display and gave the bell on the cash register a little ding. I looked up. He kind of half-smiled at me. I went all liquid inside.

"Hey," he said. His back was to the store. He couldn't see that Devin was standing up now and waving at me. I wanted to kill the guy.

"You came," I said. I didn't mean to sound so cold. I couldn't help it. I was terrified.

"I always come," Leo said. "I'm a jerk, but I always come."

I turned away. It must have seemed like I was still mad. I was really just trying to motion to Devin to get out while Leo wasn't looking.

Leo sighed. I could see his big shadow slump. "Look," he said, "I don't blame you for not wanting to see me. I admit it. I'm a bonehead. I'm an idiot. I acted like a two-year-old. I've got a jealousy problem. I've got a confidence problem. But, hey, I'm a guy. Sometimes I can't get the words out to tell you…" He sucked in his breath, "…that I'm, you know…scared, I guess. I don't want you to leave. I don't want you to give up on me. But I know if I keep on acting like I did, you will."

Leo threw his hands up in the air. "I don't know what else I can say! I'm sorry, Frances." That's when I knew how bad he felt. He always calls me Frank.

I could see Devin making fun of him in the background. He was rubbing his eyes like he was crying. He was pretending to go "boo hoo hoo." If Leo saw him, he'd never forgive me.

I'd never been that scared in my life. I clenched my teeth together so they wouldn't chatter. Leo looked at me as if he couldn't believe I was still holding out. He usually just had to turn those hazel eyes to me and I gave in pretty quickly.

"This probably won't make any difference, but I brought you something," he said. He lifted his right hand to his pocket and winced. His knuckles were all red and swollen. "I have to get a softer dashboard if I'm going to use it for a punching bag." He tried again to put his hand in his pocket, but he couldn't close it enough. "Can you get it for me?"

I nodded—but I really meant the nod for Devin. He was pointing to the bathroom and pretending to tiptoe away.

Leo lifted his arm. I leaned across the counter and slipped my hand inside his jacket. Devin acted like he was shocked at my behavior and wagged his finger at me. It brushed against a row of chips. There was this really loud crinkling sound. I cringed. Leo jerked halfway around.

I had to do something fast.

I grabbed Leo's head with my other hand. I pulled him across the counter and kissed him on the mouth.

It worked. Devin got out of the store without being seen.

And I got back with Leo.

I also got another box of pastels.

Chapter Five

The pastels Leo gave me only came from the Dollar Store, but they meant a lot to me. I knew he didn't want me to go to art college. But he gave me something to help get there anyway.

As a thank-you, I decided to draw him a picture. That Tuesday on my free period I sat behind the school and sketched the football team practicing. (Hey, he's a jock. That's the type of picture he likes.)

It was a disaster. Like I said, the pastels meant a lot to me—but they were still cheap. They broke. They smudged too much. Or they wouldn't smudge at all. I had no control over what I was putting on the paper. It was so frustrating.

I was just about to pack up my stuff when this little spray of pebbles landed on my lap.

"Don't be scared!" someone whispered.

I turned and saw Devin tiptoeing up to me.

He was going, "Easy, girl. Eeeeeeea-sy."

It was kind of funny. He was acting like I was this wild animal that could attack at any moment. I couldn't help myself. I laughed.

He plopped down beside me.

"What are *you* doing here?" he said.

"I go here."

"I didn't know that!"

"There's only one high school in town. I don't have much choice," I said. Then it dawned on me. "But you do. Why in the world would anyone come to Lockeport Rural Academy if they didn't absolutely have to?"

He shrugged. "What else is there to do around here?"

"Good point."

"Other than draw, that is."

He looked down at my picture. I really didn't want him seeing this one. I didn't want *anyone* seeing this one. I put my arm over it.

"Let's not start that again," I said.

"Oh, right. That's what got me in trouble in the first place," he said.

"Exactly."

"Okay, I won't look at your picture if you promise to tell me one thing." He tried that cheesy smile on me again.

"Deal," I said. "What?"

"Why are you using those crap pastels?"

I tried to brush it off.

"I don't know," I said, although, of course, I did know.

The truth is I was embarrassed to admit my boyfriend got them for me. I was embarrassed to admit I'd like a guy who didn't know the difference between a $2 box of pastels and a $50 box. It's terrible but true.

Devin said, "Why don't you use the ones I gave you? Your mother will thank me."

"My mother? What are you talking about?"

He pointed at my arm. When I tried to hide the picture, the pastels had come off on my sleeve. My white shirt was covered with these gross smudges. My picture of the football team was even worse. It was just a bunch of burgundy and gold blotches on a green background now.

I handed him the picture. "Sure. You can look at it all you want."

"Very interestink," he said in a German accent. "I see the passion! I see the fire! Ooops. Sorry." He turned the drawing around the other way. "I see I had it upside down!"

The expression on his face changed suddenly.

"Hey," he said in his own voice. "You know all this needs to be really good?"

I shook my head.

"Do you mind?" he asked and took what was left of my black pastel.

"Go ahead," I said. Who cared at this point?

He started drawing on my picture. He hunched his back so I couldn't see what he was doing.

After a while he said, "Yeah, this is better. Much better. What do you think?"

I looked at it and laughed. Devin had played connect-the-dots with all the burgundy football blobs and turned them into a picture of a big, black bunny with bloodshot eyes. The blue plaid splotch that had been Coach Isnor was now the bunny's tail.

"A definite improvement," I said. "It's just missing one little detail." I added bloody fangs.

"Wunderbar!" he said in his German accent again. "Together we will take the art world by storm!"

He handed me the picture. "Your signature please. It very much increases the picture's value on the international market." I signed it in purple. He signed in red.

"I will keep it always," he said with this dreamy look on his face.

It dawned on me that Kyla Swimm—my best friend and Lockeport's only other art nerd—might like him. He wasn't bad looking, and I could see her going for his weird sense of humor. I got it in my head that I should set them up.

Big mistake.

Chapter Six

I told Kyla about Devin that afternoon. I didn't exactly lie, but I didn't tell her all the gory details either. No use mentioning that I thought Devin was weird the first time I met him. That would just make her feel like I was handing her my rejects. She didn't need to know about the pastels, either. I didn't want it getting back to Leo that other guys were buying me presents too.

I told her about Tom Orser and the record-ing deal and Devin's interest in art. Kyla stopped doodling and looked at me.

"How ugly is he?" she said. She'd been set up before. She was suspicious.

"Not ugly at all," I answered.

"Well, I'm interested then," she said. "Not ugly at all means he's cuter than 97 percent of the guys around here."

My only problem now was going to be finding Devin. I didn't have a number for him. In fact, I didn't even know where he was staying.

It turned out I didn't have to track him down at all. I saw him the very next day.

I was at the town library, sprawled across one of the chairs, reading, when he came up behind me.

"Frances? Hey, what are you doing here?" He looked at my book and shook his head in amazement. "You're not going to believe this…" he said.

He was holding a scrap of paper. There was a file number written on it and a title for a book called *Strange Houses: Odd Abodes Throughout the Ages*. It was the book I was sitting there reading.

"Wow. Great minds think alike, huh?" he said.

I smiled. I had to admit it seemed like a pretty weird coincidence. I'd never even heard of the book before. I just picked it up because it sounded interesting—and here he was actually looking for it.

"So are you going to hog it?" he asked. "Or can we share?"

I said, "Share, I guess." Why not? I wouldn't have wanted Leo to see us together like that, poring over a book. It would have really bugged him. But since he never came into the library, I figured I didn't have to worry. I also needed a few minutes alone with Devin so I could bring up the Kyla thing.

Devin pulled a chair up beside mine and we flipped through the book. He seemed to know quite a bit about construction and architects and people who build weird houses. It was interesting. I like learning about new things.

I lost track of time. Suddenly it was almost five. I jumped up.

"Yikes!" I said. "I gotta go!"

He grabbed my arm. "Don't go yet! Stay until we get into the twentieth century at least."

"I can't," I said and shook his hand loose. "I've got to go to Leo's hockey tryouts."

"That sounds like fun!" he said.

For a second I was worried he was going to ask if he could come with me.

"Just kidding," he said and elbowed me. "Would you really rather sit in a freezing cold rink than a nice warm library?"

My answer of course was no, but I didn't say that.

I just said, "I don't have a choice. I promised."

I threw my stuff in my knapsack and was about to take off. I had two minutes to make it to the rink, but I stopped anyway. I didn't want to miss the chance to do my matchmaker thing.

I turned around and said, "Hey, do you want to have lunch tomorrow?"

"Yeah, sure. Sounds great!"

I was going to tell him about Kyla, but I thought that might scare him off. In a weird way, he actually seemed kind of shy.

"Do you know where D'Eon's Diner is?" I asked.

"That greasy spoon out by the fish plant? I love that place. It's so 1962!"

"Great. See you there at 12:30 then."

Devin was right. D'Eon's Diner is so 1962. I'm sure most of the décor—and all of the coleslaw—is at least that old. But Kyla and I love it. No one from the high school ever bothers to go that far for lunch, and the sea-food chowder is actually pretty good.

Kyla and I got there at about 12:15 so we could get a good booth. I sat facing the door. The seat backs are so high that I had to keep sticking my head out in the aisle to watch for Devin.

Kyla was nervous.

"Do I look all right?" she said.

She was wearing her usual mismatched Thrift Shop clothes. She had this thing tied around her head, but her hair still looked pretty wild. I mean that in a good way.

"You look fabulous, darling," I said. "Why are you so worried?"

Kyla pulled at her curls so her hair wouldn't be flat on top.

"I don't know. This guy just sounds too good to be true. Rich. Artistic. Musical. Not ugly. When would I ever find another guy like that in Lockeport?"

I felt bad then. Maybe I should have been a little more honest about Devin. It wouldn't help Kyla's chances if she acted like he was too good for her.

I didn't have time to do anything about it. Devin walked in the door carrying a big plastic bag. I called him over. He had this huge smile on his face—until he slipped into the booth and saw Kyla.

He looked at her like she was a rotting corpse or something. He actually jumped back out of the booth.

This was bad.

I tried to laugh as if it was a joke and said, "Kyla, this is Devin."

"Hi," she said. "Nice to meet you." I could tell by the look on her face that it wasn't nice at all.

"Hi," he said. He didn't look at either of us. He held his package against his chest and kind of glanced around the room. He was all fidgety. He said, "Ah, sorry. Look. I just came in to say I can't stay. Sorry. Have a good lunch. See ya." And he left.

I put this big smile on my face and turned back to Kyla.

"Well," I said. "That didn't go so well now, did it?"

"No, it was great!" Kyla said. "I think we really hit it off!" She grabbed her purse and slid out of the booth. I could tell she was going to cry.

"Kyla…" I said.

She got up and looked at me as if she hated me. "Do me a favor," she said. "Don't try setting me up again. Like, how desperate do you think I am?"

I tried to apologize, but she was really ranting by now. All the guys from the fish plant turned and stared.

"What were you thinking?" She practically spat at me. "Oh, I know. 'He may be a psycho, but he's a *single* psycho. He'd be perfect for Kyla!' Thanks for your confidence in me, Frances."

I couldn't stop her. She stormed out of the diner. She didn't even slow down to steal a handful of mints from the waitress station like she usually does.

Everyone went back to their meals. I sat in the booth and stared at the red leatherette seat. Kyla was right. What was I thinking? I should have gone with my first instinct. The one that told me Devin was not the type of guy to get mixed up with.

Chapter Seven

I headed back to school. I felt terrible. When I had a problem I could usually talk to Leo or Kyla about it. This time, I was clearly on my own.

I'd just turned onto Pleasant Point Road when I saw Devin barreling back toward me. He didn't look very happy.

"What was all that about?" he said.

"All what?" I said, although I really didn't want to know.

"What's the idea of bringing that girl to lunch with us?"

I didn't have an answer. Right then it didn't seem like such a great idea to admit I was setting him up. I sort of stood there, stunned, mumbling something about how good Deon's fish chowder is. He just carried right on.

"I don't know what got into you! We have a good time together. We hang out at the store. We hang out at the school. We hang out at the library. Things are going great. Then you ask me out—and I think, hey, we're finally getting somewhere. I arrive at our big date—and find out you've brought a friend!?! I don't get it!"

Is that what he thought? This was a date? I could have kicked myself. Why hadn't I just told him about Kyla in the first place?

"Look. I'm really sorry, Devin," I said. "I didn't mean to lead you on. I thought you'd realize it was just…" I tried to find the right word "…a friendly invitation. I mean, you *know* I have a boyfriend."

"Oh, right!" he said. "Leo. He's your boyfriend? That guy you're scared of?"

"I'm not scared of him!" I said.

"You sure looked like you were the other night!" He was practically screaming at me.

"I just didn't want him seeing you there, that's all." It sounded pretty lame.

"Oh yeah?" he said. "How come?"

"Well, I…I just didn't want Leo to get the wrong idea."

Devin laughed. "The wrong idea? Like maybe there was a little something going on between us? Some mutual attraction, maybe?"

"Yeah," I said.

"See, that's your problem, Frances. It wouldn't be giving Leo the wrong idea. It would be giving him the *right* idea. We *are* attracted to each other. You know it as well as I do."

What could I say to that? I didn't want to crush the guy. I didn't want to tell him he didn't appeal to me. I didn't want to be mean.

I just said, "Devin, I'm sorry but it's not like that. I love Leo."

"Oh, please!" he said. "You've got to stop kidding yourself. I don't know what type of weird hold this guy has over you. You have nothing in common! You and I like to do the same things. We laugh at the same things. Hey, we even picked out exactly the same book! You and Leo? You can't even agree on what movie to see!"

"What are you talking about?" I said.

"I bet you really enjoyed watching *Alien Slugfest*. That's just your type of film, isn't it?"

I got a chill. That was the movie Leo and I had rented the night before.

"Were you following me?" I could barely get the words out.

"Excuse me?" Devin looked like I'd really insulted him. "I'm not allowed to rent a movie? I'm not allowed to go into the town's one and only video store just because you're there?"

"How come I didn't see you?" Lockeport Movie Stop isn't that big a place.

Devin shook his head as if I was being totally dense. "Frances!" he said. "I was doing you a favor! I hid so that Bam-Bam, your caveman boyfriend, wouldn't catch us in the same room together! Isn't that what I'm supposed to do?"

I didn't answer. Things were getting out of hand. It seemed the more I said, the madder he got. The worst thing was that I could sort of see where he was coming from.

Sort of.

I made him hide from Leo. I hung out with him. I asked him for lunch. I didn't mean to, but maybe I was sending him mixed messages. Maybe he wasn't that crazy for thinking there was some hope there. I felt so bad for him.

"Devin," I said, "you're a nice guy. You're funny. And you're smart. I'm glad to be your friend, but that's all I can be. There's more to Leo and me than you can see. I hope you understand."

He looked away. There was this long silence.

Then he laughed and said, "Oh, I understand all right." I couldn't tell if it was a mad laugh or a sad laugh.

I touched his arm. "No hard feelings?"

He said, "I've got nothing but good

feelings for you, Frances." He handed me the plastic bag he was holding.

"Here. You can read all about them on the front page," he said.

I looked in the bag. It was a book. One of those big $80 coffee-table books on the history of art. I tried to give it back but he wouldn't let me. When he left, I opened it to the front page.

He'd written: "To Frances—and the beginning of our own long and beautiful history of art. With love always, Devin."

I felt sick. The poor guy. What could I do? I just hoped he'd get over it soon.

Chapter Eight

I hid the book under my bed. I called Kyla and patched things up with her. I went out with Leo that night and fished for herring off the wharf. We didn't catch anything. We never do. I didn't care. We had fun. And I was just so glad to have my life back to normal.

For a while anyway.

I went to school early the next morning to get ready for a test. Thank God I got there when I did. That picture Devin took of us in the store was taped to my locker. He'd blown it up to 8 x 10 and written across the top: "Thanks for some beautiful times together. XOXO Devin."

I tore it down and threw it into the bottom of my locker. All I needed was for Leo to see that. I didn't want him getting jealous again and I didn't want him getting mad at Devin either. The guy's life seemed bad enough as it was.

The whole morning I was totally freaked out by the picture. We barely knew each other. Why was Devin making such a big deal of this? And how did he find my locker?

But then as the day went on, I relaxed about it a bit. He gave me a picture. So what? It's not like he wrote "I love you madly" on it. He just said we had a nice time together. How terrible was that? I thought it might even have been Devin's way of saying goodbye. You know, "Thanks for the memories…"

Finding my locker wouldn't have been that hard either. He didn't have to do anything underhanded. He just had to ask around. Somebody would have known where it was.

Once I got my head around that, the whole thing didn't seem so creepy anymore. It just seemed kind of sad. He was obviously lonely. Why else would our little "relationship" have meant so much to him? It made me wonder if he'd ever gotten up the courage to call his father.

I bumped into Devin later that day when I took a shortcut home across the baseball field. He seemed fine. He smiled when he saw me and complimented me on my sweater, but he wasn't all over me or anything. It was just like friends talking.

Well, more like acquaintances talking.

I thanked him for the picture. He said he thought I might like it. We both nodded and wondered what to say next.

There was this awkward pause. I almost said goodbye, but I didn't want to look too anxious to get out of there. I didn't want to act like I hated him.

So I said, "Have you called your dad yet?"

"My dad?" he said. "Oh, yeah. I did."

"Great! How'd it go?"

"Tom's an amazing guy," he said and smiled.

I smiled too. Maybe this was all he needed to get back on track.

"Amazing? What do you mean?" I asked.

"He's so honest!" Devin sort of laughed. "You know, he came right out and said he never wanted to see me again! What a guy, eh?"

He smiled and shook his head like it was the best joke ever.

"I'm really sorry," I said, and I meant it.

Devin brushed it off.

"Hey, don't worry about it," he said. "I'm getting used to it. That's two people in one week who say they don't want to see me."

Ask me how terrible I felt then.

Chapter Nine

I felt trapped.

I *was* trapped. What could I do? I kept thinking "poor Devin." There was no way I was going to act like I was interested in him. I wasn't that stupid. But I couldn't kick him when he was down, either. I had to be nice to him. He didn't have anyone else.

All that week I kept running into him. He was at the library when I went to drop off my books. I saw him at the Dairy Maid when I stopped for an ice cream. He was down by the bridge when I went for a bike ride. Each time I had to walk this really fine line between being nice and too nice. It was so hard. Part of me would just curl up and die when I saw him coming, but I'd put a smile on my face anyway and try to do my best. It was really beginning to get to me.

That Friday I was at A Stitch In Time, picking up some material for an art project, when Devin walked in. It seemed strange. What was he doing in a dusty old fabric store?

"Oh, just browsing. You know," he said. "What else is there to do around here?"

How many times had I heard him say that? It was true, but it still kind of bugged me. I had to bite my tongue.

"You're lucky," I said in the nicest voice I could come up with. "At least you'll be leaving soon."

"What do you mean?" he said.

I didn't want to bring up anything about Tom telling him to get lost, but that's what I was thinking. So I said, "Don't you have to get back for that recording contract?"

"Oh, yeah. I meant to tell you," he said. "I've had second thoughts. I'm not sure music is really what I want to do with my life. I've kind of gotten into photography. I thought I'd hang around here for a while and work on it."

"You're not taking the contract?"

He shook his head.

I felt the blood run out of my face. This was the worst thing that could possibly happen. For me, because Devin would be staying here. But also for him. This sounded like a once-in-a-lifetime opportunity. He'd be crazy to pass it up.

I told him so.

"I've got other once-in-a-lifetime opportunities that are more important to me right now," he said.

I didn't ask what they were. I didn't even want to consider them. I just begged him not to turn down the recording deal.

He wouldn't listen.

He said his mind was made up. He was going to call the company that day and say thanks but no thanks.

I couldn't let that happen! The guy would be ruining his life—and mine, for that matter.

I looked at my watch. It was after 5:30. I had to go to work. I said, "Please, Devin. Don't do anything until we can talk about this. Okay?"

He smiled. He shrugged. He said, "Sure. I'd love to talk to you about it."

Now I just had to figure out what to say.

Chapter Ten

I was late. I'd forgotten some homework at school, but I didn't have time to pick it up. I had to run all the way to the store.

That was okay. I was so wound up from talking to Devin, it felt good to burn off some energy.

Mrs. Abdul was there when I arrived. She looked all puffy and gray. This pregnancy was really hard on her. I told her not to worry about tidying stuff up. She should just go. I'd take care of things.

I called and asked Leo to get my home-work from my locker. Then I braced myself for the suppertime rush.

An hour later all the Hamburger Helper was gone and I was on my own again. I started to restock the shelves and I thought about Devin.

I didn't have a clue how to make him change his mind. He was such a weird guy. I couldn't figure him out. He twisted every-thing I said. He just believed what he wanted to believe. It dawned on me that I could end up saying something that would actually make things worse. For a second there, I considered introducing him to my mother. Maybe she could talk some sense into him. Somebody had to.

I heard a customer walk in the door. I got up and went to the counter.

I couldn't believe it.

I was so surprised that I just kind of yelled "Tom!" I'd never even called him Mr. Orser before. He looked at me like I was nuts.

"Well, hello to you too," he said and put a package of diapers on the counter.

I rang them in. I had to say something to him but I didn't know how. Or what.

"Will there be anything else?" I said. I was just stalling for time.

"No," he said. "That's all."

He handed me the money. He was going to leave.

I blurted out, "Actually, there is one other thing."

"I have to buy something else?" He looked confused.

"No. No. Um. Sorry. Look." I gulped. "Well…"

"Yes?" he said. I couldn't tell if he found this amusing or irritating.

"Okay. I guess there's no easy way around this. I'm just going to come right out and say it," I said. "You have to talk to your son." I wiped my hands on my shirt. They were all sweaty.

"My son?" he said. "You must be mistaking me for someone else."

"You're Tom Orser."

"That's me. But I don't have a son."

I nodded.

"Devin told me you'd say that."

"Who's Devin?"

I nodded again.

"He told me you'd say that too."

Tom rolled his eyes. I pushed my hair off my face and just kept going. I was too far in to stop now.

"I'm sure you have your reasons for not wanting to see him. That's none of my business. I promise I won't tell anybody else about this. But you really need to talk to him now before he does something stupid. Maybe he'll listen to you."

Tom scratched his chin and looked at me.

"Please. I'm really worried about him."

"I can see you are," he said. "I appreciate your concern but, honestly, I don't have a son. Four daughters, two wives, no son. Someone's pulling your leg."

I got this sick feeling. I went, "But… but…um…"

"Go ahead. Ask anyone," he said. "You'll see."

He picked up the diapers.

"And if you do find out I have a son,

please call me. I like to know about these things."

He smiled and left.

I spent the rest of my shift in a daze. Tom didn't look like he was lying. And Tom didn't look like Devin's father either. He was dark and round. Devin was pale and skinny. They weren't related. I was sure of it.

Or was I?

I don't look like my parents. I look like my father's mother. It's one of those skip-a-generation things. Maybe it was the same with Devin and Tom.

And there was another thing that didn't sit right with me. I just couldn't believe that Devin was able to pull off that big a lie. I lie and my ears turn red. Leo lies and he starts rubbing his neck. Kyla lies and she bites her lip. You always know when someone is lying. Devin looked me right in the eye and told me Tom was his father. He didn't blink.

Was he a good liar?

Or was Tom?

Or was I just stupid?

I had no idea.

Midnight came. Mr. Abdul arrived for the nightshift, but there was no sign of Leo. I was just starting to worry when Chris Cooper, the guy from Diamond Taxi, showed up.

"Leo sent me," he said. "I'll take you home."

I figured Leo must have been having problems with his transmission again. But then I got in the cab and Chris handed me a package. It was the homework I asked Leo to get from my locker.

That picture of Devin and me was on top. Leo had stuck a stickie on it.

It said, "From now on, find your own way home."

Chapter Eleven

I couldn't sleep that night. I didn't even try. I was sad. I was mad. I was totally confused. I couldn't believe that I'd got myself into such a mess. I was only trying to be nice.

I turned on my computer. I was going to get to the bottom of this Tom and Devin thing.

I Googled Tom. There were tons of entries and they all said the same thing. Tom Orser married Marlene Nowlan, 1970. Two daughters, Jessica (born 1972) and Vivienne (born

1974). Marlene died of breast cancer, 1992. Tom married Cindy Schultz, 1995. They had the two little girls I knew.

I stared at the screen. I couldn't believe what an idiot I was. I fell for everything Devin told me.

There was no way I could find out for sure, but I knew right then that Devin was lying about the recording contract too. I bet he even made up all that stuff he told me in the library about architecture. I bet he didn't know a thing about building or music or art, for that matter.

I was so pissed off. I was so mad about the way he used me, played on my emotions, made me feel sorry for him. I felt like such a sucker.

I wanted to talk to Leo. Say I was sorry. Tell him what Devin did. I knew if I could just explain it to him, Leo would forgive me.

I couldn't phone him right then, but I could write him.

I clicked on the e-mail icon. It took forever to open. Something was downloading. I hoped it was from Leo.

It wasn't.

It was from Devin. He sent me some of the photographs he'd been taking lately.

They were all of me. Me walking to school. Me raking the yard. Me sketching at the beach. Me goofing around with the dog. Me buying a new toothbrush.

He'd written these stupid captions under them. "Your beauty inspires me." "Pretty in Pink." "Let me be your pet."

I wanted to throw up. How did he get my e-mail address? How did he know where my house was? How did he get a picture of me at the drugstore?

I knew. The guy *had* been following me. It was no coincidence I kept bumping into him. And it was no coincidence that Leo was never around when I did.

I was suddenly totally creeped out. My mind raced through everything I'd done in the last couple of weeks. What had Devin seen? Had he been listening in on my conversations? Was he looking in my window when I changed? Did he watch what Leo and I did in the car? Was he watching me right then?

The hair on the back of my neck stood up. I yanked the curtains closed. I looked around the room. He could be in the house right now. I wanted to run down the hall to my parents' room, like a little kid having a nightmare. But I was too scared to do even that.

I sat there, shaking.

I knew I was being stupid. Devin couldn't have been there. My dad had been home sick all day. No one would have got into the house without him seeing. I was safe.

I kept telling myself that. I had to relax. Everything seems scary at four o'clock in the morning. I finally pulled myself together enough to e-mail Leo. Just a short note. I was too upset to write any more. I said, "I know this looks bad. It's not what you're thinking. Let me explain. Call me. Love, Frank."

Then I went to bed.

With the lights on.

Chapter Twelve

First thing I did when I got up the next day was check my e-mail. No reply from Leo. I called his house. His mother said he was still asleep. I could tell from the tone of her voice that she knew something was up. She sounded pretty cold—but she never liked me much anyway. I asked her to get him to phone me when he woke up.

I was in the kitchen, fuming, when Dad came in. He asked what the problem was. I almost told him about Devin and the e-mailed photos and everything, but I changed my mind. Dad's not crazy about me going away to art college next year. He thinks I'm not ready to leave home, that I couldn't handle myself in the big city. Hearing about Devin would only make things worse. So I said, "Nothing." Dad just figured I was in one of my moods, I guess.

I called Kyla. Her brother said she was babysitting the Haney kids. He thought she'd taken them to Crescent Beach. I grabbed a sweater and headed out to find her. I needed to tell someone.

I shouldn't have been surprised to run into Devin on the way. I knew what he was up to by then, but I still jumped when he slid out from behind the war memorial.

He said, "Hey, Frances!" like it was some big shock that we ran into each other. "Did you get my photos?"

I nodded. That was all I could do. I was so mad I was paralyzed.

"Do you think I have any talent?"

It took me a couple of seconds to get my mouth to work.

"Oh, you have talent all right," I said. "For lying."

He gave me this "shocked and appalled" face. I almost expected him to say, "Well, I never!" like he was some rich old lady on a sitcom.

I didn't let him say anything.

I went on, "Don't even try to deny it! I talked to Tom. He doesn't know who you are. I checked on the Internet. There's no mention of you—or all those wives and kids you told me about. You're lying!"

Devin laughed. Did that ever piss me off.

"What's so funny?"

"You're so gullible!" he said. "You believe everything you read on the Internet? Of course Tom denied it! Of course he hid it! He's got all this money and he doesn't pay child support to anyone. Not a cent. You can imagine how bad that would look for some-one in his position. Do you think he could have built that nice house if he actually paid alimony?"

He was just babbling away. Saying any-thing that came into his head. Making up more stupid stories. What did he think? That I was an idiot?

"Shut up," I said. "I don't believe you."

"But you believe Tom?!?" He threw his arms up in the air. "Why do women always fall for that guy?"

"Shut up!" It all just came pouring out of me. "Quit the acting! I don't believe anything you ever told me. Not about Tom. Not about the recording contract. Not about the weather. Nothing. I don't want to listen to you anymore. I don't want to see you. Stop following me. Go home."

"This is my home now," he said. Suddenly he was talking to me like he was the youth minister at the Baptist church. He'd gone all calm and blissed out.

"Devin," I said. "I'm serious. Go home. You need help."

"I need you," he said and tried to take my hand. "And some day you'll realize you need me too."

I swatted him away.

"Don't touch me!" I said. "If you come near me again, I'll scream."

He chuckled like I was being such a silly little girl.

"I mean it!" I said. "Don't touch me. Don't call me. Don't follow me. Do me a favor. Just forget we ever met!"

"I can't do that!" he said.

I wanted to slap that stupid smile off his face.

"Sure you can!" I said. "I have!" It wasn't true, of course, but it sounded like a good way to end our little conversation.

I took off.

My heart was going *wump, wump, wump, wump, wump*. I was shaking. But I felt good too. I felt like I'd done it. Like I was finally rid of him.

I didn't even bother trying to find Kyla. I was desperate to see Leo. I was ready to do something I should have done weeks before. I was going to be totally honest with him. I was going to tell him all about Devin. Then I was going to apologize and apologize and apologize until Leo was ready to forgive me.

I tried all his usual hangouts—his house, the rink, the school, the Dairy Maid, the football field, his grandmother's, everywhere. There was no sign of him. I left messages with everyone, telling them to say I was sorry. I didn't care how pathetic that looked. I just wanted us back to being the way we were before.

The more I looked, the worse I felt. I was pretty sure Leo was avoiding me. Who could blame him? He must have hated me when he found that picture. I spent all this time telling him he had no reason to be jealous—then he gets hit with that. He probably felt like as much of a sucker as I did.

I'd pretty much given up hope of finding him by the time I got home.

Then I saw the package leaning up against the front door.

It was a bouquet of red roses, all wrapped up in pink paper. There was one of those little typewritten cards on it, the kind you get from the flower shop. It said, "We've both done things we regret. Let's work it out. XXXXX."

I was so happy.

Chapter Thirteen

I had a big smile on my face all the way to work—but it disappeared as soon as I got there.

Mrs. Abdul was leaning against the counter, groaning. The baby was coming.

She looked terrible. She was sweating and every so often she'd open her mouth as if she was going to scream, but no sound came out. It made me think I never wanted to get pregnant.

A couple of minutes later, Mr. Abdul came racing in to take her to the hospital. He told me to lock up the store when my shift was over. He wouldn't be back that night.

I was really freaked out. I hated seeing Mrs. Abdul in so much pain and I was scared there was going to be something wrong with the baby. I just hung around, chewing on the end of my hair and worrying. A couple of customers came in, but time seemed to take forever.

Then Kyla called and took my mind off the Abduls.

She didn't even say hello.

She just said, "Question: Where does Devin live?"

"I don't know."

"I do!" I could hear her doing her little victory dance. "At least I think I do. Dad was hunting with Uncle Bill and they found an old car parked out by the radio tower. They said this pale, skinny kid was staying there. He acted all strange when they tried to find out what he was up to. I immediately thought 'Devin!' Who else would be crazy enough to hang out in the woods during hunting season?"

"It doesn't surprise me," I said. Although it actually did. Devin told me he hitchhiked here. Why would he lie about having a car? I was starting to think he'd lie about anything.

"That's not all. The guy told Dad he was a biologist doing field research. He claimed his baby blue 1994 Fiesta was his mobile lab." Kyla snorted. "Even my dad isn't stunned enough to fall for that. Can you believe that guy?"

"No," I said. "I can't. Not anymore, at least."

Then I told her all about Devin and the Google search and the pictures of me at the beach and everything. For a while I had to put up with some snarky comments from Kyla like "Oh, well, I can see why you thought Devin would be perfect for me!" But she came around.

She loved the part about me telling Devin off. She was cracking up. Apart from my little brother, I never tell anyone off.

She was enjoying it too much. I tried to distract her.

"Yeah, well, it was a day of many important firsts for me," I said. "I yelled at someone, and I got roses from Leo!"

"Yeah, right," Kyla said. "Now I know you're hallucinating. Leo's a nice guy, but he doesn't do flowers."

"Well, he did today!" I was almost singing. "He even added a little note." I recited it from memory. "'We've both done things we regret. Let's work it out. XXXXX.'"

"XXXXX?" Kyla said. "C'mon, Frances. Leo doesn't do kissy-kissy either."

I said, "What are you saying?" although I didn't really need to ask.

"Yoo-hoo! Time to wake up!" She said it in her crazy-old-lady voice. "Those roses are from Devin."

I tried to deny it. I argued with her. But I knew she was right. I bet, somewhere inside, I knew the flowers were from Devin all along. I just didn't want it to be true.

All I really, really wanted was for the guy to get out of my life. He was like a stain or a rash or a wart that you just can't get rid of.

I didn't know what more I could do. I'd told him to go away. I'd told him to leave me alone. How much clearer could I have been? Why was he still bugging me? Couldn't he get it through his thick skull that I didn't like him?

Kyla said, "You've got a stalker on your hands, Frances."

That's not what I wanted to hear. It really annoyed me. Typical Kyla, I thought. Always blowing things way out of proportion. Anything for a good story.

"Quit exaggerating, Kyla. It's bad enough as it is."

"I'd call the cops if I were you."

"Oh, please! And tell them what?" I said. "'He gave me flowers. Arrest him!' Sure."

"What about him taking those pictures of you?" she said.

"There's no law against that either. It's not like I was naked or anything," I said.

"I don't know, Fran. I don't like the sound of this guy. He makes up stories. He follows you. He won't take no for an answer. There's something wrong with him."

"Duh! Obviously. But being nuts isn't illegal."

"Yeah, but that doesn't mean it isn't dangerous," Kyla said. "At least according to my bible."

She meant *People Magazine*. She's a junkie.

"I read this article a little while ago about celebrity stalkers. The guy in it said something like 'Sure, they're crazy—but crazy isn't stupid.' That's what makes them so dangerous. Stalkers are insane *and smart*."

"I could say that about you, Kyla. But I wouldn't have you arrested. Unless you don't quit it, that is."

"I'd be worried, Fran. Who knows? Devin could get violent."

"Shut up!" I said. "Now you're just trying to scare me."

"I'm not," she said. "I'm just warning you."

"Look, the guy's not a stalker. He's just pathetic. He's never done anything violent.

And anyway, even if he did, I'm a big girl. I could probably take him."

Kyla started laughing.

"Oh, right! There's a fight I'd *love* to see. Devin the Creep versus Frances the Klutz."

She was howling. She could barely catch her breath. Kyla knows what a spaz I am.

"I can just picture the two of you, flailing away at each other! It would be better than the WWF. No! NO! I'm wrong! It would *be* the WWF. By which, of course, I mean the Weirdo Wrestling Federation! We'll get Devin a cape and a mullet, and we'll get you one of those little silver leotards and a boob job. You'll make millions."

It was so stupid I had to laugh too.

After the day I'd had, I needed it.

And the day wasn't over yet.

Chapter Fourteen

Mr. Abdul called at about nine o'clock that night to say he had a brand new-daughter. I tried to sound happy, but I didn't do a very good job. I was so bummed out about Leo and the picture and the flowers.

I tried to call him, but there was no one home.

I could have screamed. I wanted to kill Devin for screwing up my life. I kept thinking about what I was going to do the next time I saw him.

I was going to tell him that he was repulsive and disgusting and sick and perverted. I was going to say he smelled bad. I was going to threaten to call the cops. I was going to say whatever it took to get rid of him for good.

That was my plan, anyway.

It started to pour at about ten o'clock. With all that rain, the customers pretty much stopped coming. To keep myself busy, I drew a little card for the baby. I was tired and cranky so it wasn't very creative. I just sketched a picture of the harbor and wrote "Welcome to Lockeport's newest citizen!"

That took me until about 10:30. I still had an hour and a half to go. I figured Mr. Abdul was going to be tired the next day. I decided to help out by unloading some stock in the back room for him.

I knew something was wrong as soon as I walked in.

I smelled roast chicken.

Chapter Fifteen

"Frances! You surprised me!"

Devin was standing in the back room, holding a couple of wineglasses and trying to look cool. Beside him was a big cardboard box set up like a supper table. It had two place settings, a candle, a carving knife, a take-out salad and one of those little roast chickens you buy in the grocery store.

Devin put the wineglasses on the "table" and waved me away.

"Go back! Go back!" he said. "I'm not ready for you yet."

All that stuff I was going to say to him? I totally forgot it. I just stood there with my hand on my chest and my heart going crazy.

"How did you get in here?" I said.

"Fran-cessss," he went, like I was being stupid. "The bathroom window! You were the one who showed it to me. Remember? Our second night together?"

He was doing that romantic thing again. I couldn't stand it.

"Get out of here!" I said.

"What?!" He was laughing. "We haven't even eaten yet!"

"Get out!" I said. "You're not allowed in here."

"I'm not allowed in a store? Frances, how do you expect Mr. Abdul to make any money if you won't let the customers in?"

He winked at me. He thought he was so clever.

"You're not a customer," I said. "I'm calling the cops!"

I turned. He grabbed my arm and swung me back around.

"Whoa. Whoa. Whoa," he said. "Hold on. I wouldn't want you to do something you'll regret. Not again."

"What are you talking about?!?"

"C'mon! You know we both did things in the past that we're not very proud of. That's why I'm here! To patch things up. I thought if we had a nice little dinner, just the two of us, we could put bygones behind us. You know, make up. Move on."

He pulled me in close like he was going to kiss me. I turned my head and pushed him away. He held on.

I said, "Trust me! I haven't done anything I regret! I meant everything I said. Now let go of me!"

I punched him in the chest. He barely flinched. I kicked his shins. He just said, "Frances, calm down!"

I went nuts. I screamed. I kicked. I pushed. I pulled. I slapped him. I had to get away.

He hit me across the face. I couldn't believe how strong he was.

My head flew back. My glasses rammed into my nose. I was stunned. No one had ever hit me before.

I stopped struggling. I couldn't move.

"Sorry, Frances," he said and rubbed my cheek with his fingertips. "All better now?"

He looked me right in the eye, as if he was really concerned. As if I'd had a seizure and he only hit me because he had to.

My arm hurt where he held it. It dawned on me that I'd have a bruise the next day.

I tried to smile back. I didn't want him to hit me again.

I swallowed and said, "Devin, you better go before Mr. Abdul gets here. I'm not allowed to let customers in the back room."

"Did you forget?" He laughed. "Mr. Abdul's not coming back tonight! We're safe."

I wondered how he knew that. How long had he been there? How much had he heard?

I tried something else.

"Leo will be here soon," I said. "He gets jealous. He's a big guy."

Devin stroked my hair. "You don't have to worry about him, Frances. He knows about us now. He won't be bothering you anymore."

"But…but there'll be customers. I've got to be out front for the customers." My voice was shaking and I could barely keep from crying.

"You're right!" Devin said. "I forgot about that!"

He led me back into the store. He had his arm around my waist like we were in love. He stank of sweat and too much aftershave.

He locked the door and flipped the sign to "Closed."

"There," he said. "Now we won't have to worry about customers either. I'm sure Mr. Abdul won't mind you closing up a little early, this being a special occasion and all."

I could feel myself filling up with panic. It was like someone put it in a needle and shot it in my veins. I was losing control. And hope.

I looked out the window. A car drove by. I threw my free arm up and waved wildly. I screamed, "Help! Help!"

Devin switched off the lights. The car didn't even slow down.

"This is kind of nice," he said, "being alone in the dark. Now, c'mon, Frances. Our dinner's getting cold."

The only light in the store came from the Highway Buyway sign. It made Devin's face look almost green. It reminded me of a horror movie.

"You don't know how long I've waited for this moment," he said.

He took me back into the stockroom.

Chapter Sixteen

Devin pulled up a box for me to sit on. He lit the candle and sat down opposite me, blocking the way into the store.

I thought of the bathroom window. I'd have to climb onto the back of the toilet, then wiggle out. I'd never be able to do it in time.

"You look beautiful," he said. He didn't seem to notice that I was crying.

"Champagne, dahling?" he asked. I didn't answer. He pulled a bottle out from somewhere and poured us each a wineglass full.

"To our undying love!" He raised his glass. "C'mon, Frances." He made me lift my glass. "To us!"

He threw his champagne back in one big gulp. I took a sip. It stung, and I knew he'd split my lip when he hit me.

He said, "I have to apologize to you." For a second I thought there was a chance. I thought he might let me go.

But he just said, "I don't have much money since I turned down that record deal. A number of publishers are interested in my photographs, but until I decide which one I want to sign with, I'm going to be a little short of cash. I hope you'll understand."

He put his hand on mine. I didn't pull it away. I just tightened up inside.

"You deserve more than this," he said. "Some day I'll make sure you have it. Until then, will you accept this as a token of my love?"

He put a gift on the table. I just stared at it.

"Open it," he said.

I didn't move.

"Open it!" he screamed. Before I could do anything, he grabbed it and tore the paper off. He was like a crazy man.

"Look, I am trying, Frances! What more can I do? Is this not good enough? Is that the problem?"

He slammed a full set of charcoal pencils on the table. The plates jumped and rattled.

"I know it's not a diamond ring! I apologized for that! But I thought you'd like it anyway!" He glared at me.

"I do like it!" I said. I was whimpering. I had my head down. I couldn't look at him. "I do. The pencils are beautiful…They're the best…They must have cost a lot. Thank you very much. "

"I hope you'll draw something for me with them," he said. When I looked up, he was smiling. "Now how about some food?"

I nodded. He began to carve the chicken. I realized he could kill me with that knife.

Or I could kill him.

"More champagne?" I said.

Chapter Seventeen

"Of course!"

I filled his glass. He took a big swig and began to carve again. I watched him as he sliced into the breast, cut off a leg.

"White or dark?" he said.

"You help yourself." I smiled. "I'll get my own."

"No, no, no," he said. "You're my guest. White or dark?"

He filled my plate, then served himself. I suggested another toast.

"To your big publishing deal!" I said.

He smiled and tossed back his glass of champagne. I went to refill it. I wanted him drunk and sloppy.

He stopped me.

"No more for me, thanks. I don't want to miss a moment of our night together." He kissed my hand. "I have big plans for us."

He gave me a slow smile. My skin crawled. I sucked in my breath.

"Don't be nervous," he said. "We'll take it easy."

No, I thought, no. I'm not going to let that happen.

I lurched across the table. I tried to grab the carving knife, but he was faster. He got it first.

"Now, Frances," he said.

That's what I was thinking too, only to me it sounded like "*Now*, Frances!" Go for it!

I grabbed the chicken carcass and flung it at his head. He ducked. I missed. But it gave me a couple of extra seconds to get away. I jumped over the table.

Or tried to anyway.

I really am a spaz. My back leg hit the box on the way past and everything went flying. Glasses smashed. The candle went out. Devin swore. He lunged at me.

He caught the back of my sweater. He slipped on the chicken grease and pulled us both down. I kicked him in the head. I got away.

I ran blindly into the store, sliding in my greasy shoes, knocking cans onto the floor, ramming into shelves. I fumbled for the phone. I picked up the receiver. I could feel Devin right behind me.

I dialed nine, one...

His hand slammed the phone down.

"I hoped it wouldn't come to this," he said.

He brought the carving knife up to my throat.

Chapter Eighteen

He had my hair in one hand and the knife in the other. He was pulling me back to the stockroom. He was saying something to me, but I wasn't listening.

I was praying. Not to God. I don't know who that is. I was just praying. "Please help me. Please. Please. Please." Over and over and over again. I was hoping somehow that Dad or Leo or Kyla or someone would pick up my radio waves and come get me. With the knife to my throat, it was all I could do. Hope.

I wanted to believe it would work, but I'm not that stupid. No one was coming for me. Mr. Abdul was at the hospital. Dad was asleep in front of the TV. Leo was…I didn't know where Leo was. I just knew he wasn't coming for me.

Once I realized that, the weirdest thing happened. I felt almost calm. Not calm in a happy way, of course. But calm, like the way you feel when you realize there's nothing more you can do. I think the word for it is "resigned."

I knew it was all over.

I thought about Devin. I realized I should have figured him out earlier. That story about Tom Orser? If I'd done the math, I'd have known he didn't have time to have all those kids. The recording deal? I just had to look at Devin's clothes to realize he didn't have any money. Us choosing exactly the same book? Yeah, right. He'd been in the library, spying on me. I bet he saw what book I was reading and then went looking for the file number.

I felt sad that I hadn't been smarter.

It seemed like such a waste, to die at seventeen.

I felt sad for my mother. We'd gone through some rough patches, but we were still really close. I knew she was excited about me going to art college. I was getting to do something she'd always wanted to do. Now neither of us would go.

I felt sad for my father. He'd blame himself. He didn't like me working alone at a convenience store out on the highway. He'd tried to stop me, but I'd won. We both knew he didn't make enough money to pay for my college education. Somebody had to.

I felt sad for my brother, too. I should have been nicer to him. He wasn't that bad. All fourteen-year-old boys are irritating. He couldn't help it. Now I was going to die and really screw up his life. With me dead, there was no way my parents would let him do anything. They'd watch him like a hawk. They'd worry about him all the time.

I even felt kind of sad for Kyla. She was going to be all alone. No one else in Lockeport really got what was so great about her.

Devin pushed me down on one of the cardboard boxes. My back was against the wall. He stuck the tip of the knife under my chin. I had to lift my head so it wouldn't cut me.

He was still talking, but now tears were rolling down his face.

"I wanted this to work out so badly," he said. "We have the type of love that only comes along once in a lifetime, but you threw it away! Like it was a wad of Kleenex you blew your nose into. Like it was something stuck to the bottom of your shoe! And why? I asked myself that over and over. You used to feel the love between us. I saw it in your eyes, right from our first night together. Then Leo went and poisoned your mind against me."

He turned the knife. I felt a little pinch and then something trickling down my neck. He gently wiped the blood away with his index finger and shook his head.

"I thought I could help you. I thought if I just gave it time. But you're too far gone. I can see that. I don't have any choice."

He twisted up his face to stop crying. A groan came out of him as if he was pushing something really heavy. Or like he was in pain.

"I'm sorry," I said. Believe it or not, right then I did feel sorry for him. No one loved him. That was the only thing I knew for sure about his life.

"Sorry's not enough, Frances. I need more. I need to have you."

"You can't have me," I said. I wasn't screaming or mad or anything. I was just telling him the truth.

He nodded.

"Then I have to kill you," he said.

Chapter Nineteen

It was that word. "Kill." It did something to me. It was so much worse than "die."

"I *have* to kill you," he said again. "Then I'll have to kill myself. I can't live without you."

He shrugged.

"At least that way we'll be together for all time."

He smiled at me, like a guy just trying to make the best of a bad situation.

"Do you mind if I have another drink first?" he asked.

I shook my head, but not too much. The knife was still there. I realized I didn't want it cutting me.

"Before I die," I said, "there's something I'd like to do."

"What's that?" he said. He was struggling to pour the champagne with one hand.

"I'd like to draw your picture."

I could tell he was surprised. He stopped pouring and looked at me.

I took as deep a breath as I could without moving the knife.

"You're very handsome," I said. "And… and you've done so much in your short life. Music…Photography…"

He chewed on his lip and studied me. It's like he wanted to see right into me. I tried to make my eyes smile.

"I know things haven't gone well between the two of us. And…and maybe it has to end this way. But that doesn't mean you should just be forgotten. There should be something to remember you by. Like a portrait," I said.

"I know you better than anybody else. I think I could capture what's special about you."

He pulled the knife away, but he was still hesitating.

"There are a lot of murder-suicides these days," I said. "We'd probably just be another. But if there were a hand-drawn portrait of the killer…by the victim…that would be different. The newspapers might really pick up on it."

He tilted his head.

"Maybe the TV stations too. With your music background, it could even interest *Entertainment Tonight*."

There was nothing else I could say. I waited.

"You're right," he said. "That might get some interest."

He looked around.

"Do you have any paper?"

"Yeah, I've got lots," I said. I didn't want to give him a chance to change his mind. I just tore a big jagged sheet of brown paper off a packing crate. I could tell he didn't like the look of it much.

"I love the rugged quality of this paper, don't you?" I said and rubbed my hand along it, like it was just the thing I was looking for.

"Ah. Yeah," he said. "It's great. So how do you want me to sit?"

He turned his head to the side. He stared off into the distance. He'd obviously seen lots of paintings of famous people.

"Is this okay?"

"That's perfect," I said. "Now don't move."

I opened my new box of charcoal pencils. I chose a 2B because it had the sharpest point. I looked at Devin. His features were actually pretty nice. A straight nose. Good cheekbones. Almond-shaped eyes. He could have been handsome if someone different had been behind that face.

I sketched an oval, roughed in a nose and eyes. I held the pencil upright in front of his face.

He flinched.

"Sorry. I'm just making sure I get the proportions right," I said.

"Yeah, yeah. I know," he said. He always had to act like he knew.

I drew the mouth, adjusted the nose. I looked at the drawing. Even at that early stage, I could see Devin in it. It's amazing what you can do when you concentrate.

I raised the pencil again. He thought I was just checking proportions. He didn't flinch.

Not until I rammed the pencil right up his left nostril.

He fell to the floor, screaming, blood spurting everywhere.

I ran past him, through the store, out the front door.

It was just before midnight.

And Leo was pulling into the parking lot.

Epilogue

Devin Orser's real name is Dwayne Parker. He doesn't play an instrument. He knows nothing about art. Or architecture. Or biology.

His father wasn't Tom Orser, but Donnie Parker did leave the family when Devin was eight. His mother thinks that's what happened to him.

Kyla was right. Devin is crazy, but he isn't stupid. She knew he was trouble. That's why she sent Leo for me as soon as she saw the baby blue Fiesta parked behind the Highway Buyway.

Devin goes to court next Thursday for stalking, kidnapping and attempted murder. Of course he says it's all just a big misunderstanding. A lover's quarrel. Devin knows in his heart that we'll be together again soon.

That's why I wake up screaming every night.

I still want to go away to art college. And I will. I won't let Devin take that away from me.

But I have to admit, I'm scared. Maybe I should just stay in Lockeport for a while with Mom and Dad.

And Leo.

We'll see.

OTHER TITLES IN THE ORCA SOUNDINGS SERIES